oct.2

Ruck

My Favorite Machines

Trucks

Colleen Ruck

A⁺

Smart Apple Media

Smart Apple Media
P.O. Box 3263, Mankato, MN 56002

 An Appleseed Editions book

Planning and production by Discovery Books Limited
Designed by D.R ink
Edited by Colleen Ruck

Library of Congress Cataloging-in-Publication Data
Ruck, Colleen.
Trucks / by Colleen Ruck.
   p. cm. -- (My favorite machines)
Includes index.
ISBN 978-1-59920-680-6 (library binding)
1. Trucks--Juvenile literature. I. Title.
TL230.15.R86 2012
388.3'44--dc22
                              2011010303

Photograph acknowledgments
Shutterstock: pp. 4 (egd), 5 (James Steidl), 6 bottom (R. Carner), 8 (Vibrant Image Studio), 9, 10 top (Dmitry Kalinovsky), 10 bottom, (Max Blain), 11 (Jarvier Sanchez), 12 (Mark III Photonics), 13 (Vibrant Image Studio), 14 (Susan Law Cain), 15 (501room), 16 (mikeledray), 17 (DESmith Photography), 18 (Vadim Koziosky), 19 (Cary Kalscheuer), 20 (Nadezha Bolotina), 21 (Philip Lange), 22 (Ivaschenko Roman); Side Dump Industries: p. 23 (Peter Laskie/JD Gordon Advertising); Volvo Trucks: pp. 6 top, 7.

Cover photo: Shutterstock (akva)

Printed in the United States of America at Corporate Graphics
In North Mankato, Minnesota

DAD0502
52011

9 8 7 6 5 4 3 2 1

Contents

Trucks Everywhere

Trucks are huge, powerful machines. They carry heavy loads.

Trucks have a cab at the front
and a trailer at the back.

Trailer

Cab

5

The Cab

The controls are in the cab. The driver sits in the cab to drive the truck.

Some truck drivers spend days on the road. They have a bed in their cab so they can stop and sleep.

Tankers

Tankers are trucks with big, round trailers. They carry liquids such as milk or **gasoline**.

This truck carries **concrete** in a huge drum. The drum spins to mix the concrete and keep it liquid until it is needed.

Different Trucks

Some trucks come in one piece.

Some have a cab that can be separated from the trailer.

This truck can **tow** three trailers.
It is called a road train.

Carrying Cars

Some trucks are **designed** to carry cars. The cars sit on ramps called decks.

The cars are strapped down so they do not roll off.

Cranes

This truck has a **crane** on its trailer. The arms of some cranes can reach more than 300 feet (100 meters). That is as long as a soccer field!

This truck has a **cherry picker** on its trailer. It is being used to fix **power lines**.

Fire Trucks

Fire trucks rush to fires with their **sirens** wailing.

This fire truck has
an extra-long ladder
to reach the top
of high buildings.

Garbage Trucks

All the trash you throw away at home is collected by a garbage truck.

Another truck picks up trash that can be **recycled**.

Off-road Trucks

Off-road trucks are great for driving over rough, bumpy ground. They can even go through water.

This off-road truck is taking part in a **rally** race.

Dump Trucks

Dump trucks carry heavy dirt, sand, and rocks. This truck tips up to empty dirt out of the back.

This dump truck tips sideways to empty its load of rocks.

Glossary

cherry picker   A traveling crane designed to carry a person in a bucket at the end of its arm.

concrete   A material used for making roads and buildings.

crane   A machine that moves heavy things by lifting them in the air.

designed   Made for a job.

gasoline   Fuel used in cars and some trucks.

power lines   Cables that carry electricity.

siren   An alarm.

tow   To pull.

rally   A race for trucks and cars over roads and tracks.

recycle   To use again.

Web sites

Index